INFORMATION
EXPLORER
JUNIOR

Play It Safe Online

by Phyllis Cornwall

CHERRY LAKE PUBLISHING · ANN ARBOR, MICHIGAN

A NOTE TO PARENTS AND TEACHERS: Please remind your children how to stay safe online before they do the activities in this book.

CHERRY LAKE Publishing

A NOTE TO KIDS: Always remember your safety comes first!

Published in the United States of America
by Cherry Lake Publishing
Ann Arbor, Michigan
www.cherrylakepublishing.com

Content Adviser: Gail Dickinson, PhD, Associate Professor, Old Dominion University

Book design and illustration: The Design Lab

Photo credits: Cover, ©iStockphoto.com/monkeybusinessimages; page 5, ©Monkey Business Images/Shutterstock, Inc.; page 10, ©Dmitriy Shironosov/Shutterstock, Inc.; page 12, ©Rmarmion/Dreamstime.com; page 15, ©R. Gino Santa Maria/ Shutterstock, Inc.; page 16, ©Lisa F. Young/Shutterstock, Inc.; page 17, ©Fred Sweet/ Shutterstock, Inc.; page 20, ©Marcelmooij/Dreamstime.com; page 21, ©Elena Elisseeva/Dreamstime.com

Library of Congress Cataloging-in-Publication Data
Cornwall, Phyllis.
  Play it safe online / by Phyllis Cornwall.
    p. cm. — (Information explorer junior)
  Includes bibliographical references and index.
  ISBN 978-1-61080-364-9 (lib. bdg.)—ISBN 978-1-61080-373-1 (e-book)—
ISBN 978-1-61080-389-2 (pbk.)
1. Internet—Safety measures—Juvenile literature. I. Title.
  TK5105.875.I57C669 2012
  004.67'80289—dc23   2011034507

Cherry Lake Publishing would like to acknowledge
the work of The Partnership for 21st Century Skills.
Please visit www.21stcenturyskills.org for more information.

Printed in the United States of America
Corporate Graphics Inc.
January 2012
CLSP10

Table of Contents

CHAPTER ONE

Online Safety Rules

Do you practice safety? Do you know what that means? Practicing safety means not doing things that could hurt you or others. It means staying away from danger. There are different kinds of dangers, even when you use a computer. In this book, we are going to explore **online** safety.

Be careful when you go online.

Everyone has to follow rules in the school lunchroom.

Your school has safety rules that you are expected to follow. Not running in the halls is one of these rules. Not cheating and not damaging school property are others. These rules help students get along with each other. They also help prevent people from getting hurt in some way.

Your school has computer rules, too. You probably signed a form called an **Acceptable Use Policy**. It lists rules you are expected to follow when you are using school computers. You can't mess with other kids' computer files. You can't download anything without permission. When you signed the form, you were promising to follow these rules. These rules will keep you safe on the computer.

Did you sign the Acceptable Use Policy? Have you ever seen it? The media specialist or a teacher can show it to you. Is it too hard to understand? Ask an adult to help you.

Read your Acceptable Use Policy carefully.

Acceptable Use Policy

To get a copy of this activity, visit www.cherrylakepublishing.com/activities.

Activity

Make an Acceptable Use Policy for your computer at home. Write a list of rules for you and your family to follow. You can look at your school's policy for ideas. Should you ask for permission before going online? Maybe you should limit your time on the computer. Type up your list on the computer. Print it out. Ask your family members to sign the paper. You sign it too! Post it near your family computer. Then everyone will see the safety rules.

Make sure everyone follows the rules.

CHAPTER TWO

Online Privacy

Today at school, the MOST EMBARRASSING thing happened...

It is easy to keep other people from reading your journal.

Privacy means keeping some things to yourself. The words you write in a journal are your own thoughts and personal information. You probably don't want to share them with other people. The things other people tell you are their private thoughts and information. You should not share them with anyone else.

When you are online, you are connected to many other people. Strangers can read your words and see pictures that you post on the **Internet**. Your friends or family might be embarrassed or get into trouble if you post pictures of them or things they said. Don't post their e-mail address, home address, or the school they attend. Strangers may try to find them. Doing these things is not practicing online safety.

Passwords help protect your information.

CAUTION! Don't be tricked. People don't always tell the truth online. Sometimes they pretend they are someone else. Sometimes they pretend to be nice. You can't tell by reading their words. You shouldn't trust them. They might be dishonest or dangerous. Keep your personal information private. That will protect you from pretenders.

You never know who will read the things you post online.

Strangers aren't the only ones who can harm you. Even people you know can cause trouble. They can see your words and pictures. Maybe you wrote about yourself. Maybe you wrote about your family, your friends, or your teachers. People might use your words to embarrass you. They might try to get you into trouble. Writing on the Internet is public. Even places you think are private are not. Be very careful about what you write. It might come back to hurt you.

To get a copy of this activity, visit www.cherrylakepublishing.com/activities.

Activity

Some information is safe to share. Other information is not. Can you tell which is which? Look at the list below. Are these things safe to share online?

1. Your favorite color
2. Where you go to school
3. What you had for dinner last night
4. Your birthday
5. Your name

ANSWERS: 1. safe, 2. not safe; a stranger could use this to find you, 3. safe, 4. not safe; a stranger could use this to figure out who you are, 5. not safe; never use your real name, especially when you don't know who will read or see what you post.

CHAPTER THREE

Safe Places Online

The Internet can be a fun and safe place to play and learn. But how do kids find safe places on the Internet? After all, unsafe places don't have warning signs! You will

Ask a parent or a teacher to help you look for the Terms of Use and Privacy Policies on your favorite Web sites.

12

have to use your common sense and follow some simple tips.

Know where to look for safe Web sites. At school, your teacher can suggest some sites. So can your media specialist and the public library. Libraries often have **databases**. These are kid-friendly, safe, and **reliable**. There are also many **search engines** just for kids. These will help you find safe sites. Two popular search engines are *www.kidsclick.org* and *http://kids.yahoo.com.*

At home, always tell your parent or guardian when you'll be surfing the Internet. Make a list of each site you visit and show them the list. If you see anything online that upsets you, turn off the screen and tell your parent immediately. There's lots of information online. Not all of it is for kids.

Stay safe when you are online.

To get a copy of this activity, visit www.cherrylakepublishing.com/activities.

Activity

You can **bookmark** your favorite Web sites. This makes it easy for you to find them later.

1. Find a Web site that you like. Make sure it is kid-friendly. Ask an adult if you are not sure.
2. Go to the site. Push the Control or Command key and the D key on your keyboard at the same time.
3. Click "Add" or "Done" on the menu that pops up, or just hit Enter on your keyboard.
4. Now find your bookmark. It might be at the top of your screen under "Bookmarks" or "Favorites." You might see it at the top of the window that shows the Web site. Click the name of the site you just bookmarked.
What happens?

CHAPTER FOUR

Staying Safe Online

Dangerous places have warning signs. They let you know to be careful. "Wet Floor" signs keep you from slipping. "No Diving" signs keep you from diving into shallow

Warning signs help keep people safe.

water. Unsafe places on the Internet don't have warning signs. You have to use your common sense. That will keep you safe.

Many Web sites have rules to follow. Those rules are found on the Web site. They are on the site's **Terms of Use** and **Privacy Policy**

Teachers and media specialists can help you find safe and interesting Web sites.

Databases often have information that is hard to find elsewhere.

page. Your parents and teachers can help you find these rules. Some popular sites have rules about age. They say users must be at least 13 years old. Those sites may want you to become a member. You might have to create an account. Ask your parent for permission before you create one.

To get a copy of this activity, visit www.cherrylakepublishing.com/activities.

Activity

Passwords are important. They protect your account from other people. Can you create a password that follows these rules?:

1. At least 8 letters and numbers long
2. A mix of letters and numbers
3. Does not include your name, age, pet's name, or anything else that someone could guess

Try making a sentence. Turn it into a password using the first letter from each word in the sentence. Replace some of the letters or words with numbers. For example, "The dog liked to leave the house before me," could be "TDL2LTHB4M." Make sure it is something you can remember!

Always ask permission before creating an account.

Advertisements try to trick you into clicking on them.

Have you seen **advertisements** on Web sites? They are on the top or sides of pages. Sometimes they surprise you by popping up. They might be bright and colorful. They might say "You Won a Prize!" What happens if you click on them? You will end up at an advertiser's Web site. Don't be fooled. Don't click on these ads.

You can have lots of fun online. You can learn many things. Do you have friends or family who are far away? You can talk to them online. You can write stories. You can make movies. You can safely do all this and more. Just use the safety tips in this book. Have fun!

There are many fun things to see and do on the Internet.

Does a Web site make you uncomfortable? Does an advertisement make you feel unsafe? Tell a trusted adult. That person will help you get out of it. You will learn how not to go there again.

Glossary

Acceptable Use Policy (ak-SEP-tuh-buhl YOOSS PAH-luh-see) rules that restrict how technology may be used

advertisements (AD-ver-tize-muhnts) paid announcements meant to sell something

bookmark (BUK-mark) a Web site address stored on a computer so that the user can easily return to the site later

databases (DAY-tuh-bays-ez) sets of related information that are grouped together in one location in a computer

Internet (IN-tur-net) the electronic network that allows millions of computers around the world to connect together

online (ON-line) connected to other computers through the Internet

privacy (PRYE-vuh-see) the freedom from having others know your thoughts or read your words

Privacy Policy (PRYE-vuh-see PAH-luh-see) a statement of how a Web site shares or collects information about visitors

reliable (ri-LYE-uh-buhl) trustworthy or dependable

search engines (SURCH EN-juhnz) computer programs that help you find words or information you request

Terms of Use (TURMZ UHV YOOSS) a collection of rules for using a Web site and reasons why your access to a site can be discontinued

Find Out More

BOOKS

Curatola Knowles, Carmela N. *Piano and Laylee Go Online.* Eugene, OR: International Society for Technology in Education, 2011.

Oxlade, Chris. *My First Internet Guide.* Chicago: Heinemann Educational Books, 2007.

WEB SITES

National Crime Prevention Council—Stay Safe Online
www.mcgruff.org/#/Advice/http://www.mcgruff.org/advice/online-safety/stay-safe-online
McGruff the Crime Dog teaches sensible safety tips with colorful animations on this fun, educational site.

TeacherVision
www.teachervision.fen.com/educational-technology/printable/6024.html
Read and print out a copy of an Acceptable Use Policy.

Index

About the Author

Phyllis Cornwall is a media specialist in Michigan. She loves encouraging her students to use online resources in fun, considerate, and safe ways. When not at school, she enjoys spending time with her expanding family, which now includes Samantha.